All-Color G

American Birds

by Roland C. Clement

A Ridge Press Book

BANTAM BOOKS
TORONTO · NEW YORK · LONDON · SYDNEY

Photo Credits

All photographs from National Audubon Society.
Arthur W. Ambler: 35, 36, 66, 129, 138, 148. Peggy Amerson: 119. Gerry Atwell: 106. Alfred Bailey: 121. Ken Brate: 136, 145. Ed Cesar: 88-89. Stephen Collins: 93 left, 123, 142, 151, 152, 154 right. Allan D. Cruickshank: 24-25, 55, 56, 65, 67, 69, 72, 90, 116, 122, 125, 126, 133, 135, 144, 147. Helen Cruickshank: 22-23, 26, 30, 32, 54, 71, 76-77, 86-87, 94-95, 96, 104, 108, 134. Thase Daniel: 28-29, 34, 37, 44, 46, 79, 81, 84, 110, 114, 115, 120, 137, 146, 149, 150, 153. Treat Davidson: 156. Harry Engels: 60, 92. Robert J. Erwin: 62-63, 99. Kenneth W. Fink: 31. John H. Gerard: 48-49, 74, 102, 105, 117, 155. Woodrow Goodpaster: 100, 101, 124. S. A. Grimes: 132. C. O. Harris: 45. Robert C. Hermes: 52-53, 57, 103. Edwin J. Howard: 93 right. Ray Hunold: 61, 131. William Jahoda: 109, 111. Paul Johnsgard: 38, 39, 40, 41. B. E. Johnson: 33. Henry C. Johnson: 86-87. Fred Lahrman: 58-59, 68. H. Charles Laun: 20-21. Jesse Lunger: 113. Karl H. Maslowski: 42-43. Paul Nesbit: 107, 139. Charles C. Ott: 82. James F. Parnell: 143. Roger T. Peterson: 70. O. S. Pettingill, Jr.: 98, 130, 141. Bill Reasons: 51. Bucky Reeves: 50, 154 left. Leonard Lee Rue: 27. Alvin E. Staffan: 97, 112, 118, 127, 128. C. J. Stine: 73. H. A. Thornhill: 47, 83. L. F. Wanlass: 140.
Front Cover: Female Cardinal, G. Harrison (Bruce Coleman, Inc.)
Back Cover: Eastern Meadowlark, R. Carr (Bruce Coleman, Inc.)
Title Page: Grebe, Helen Cruickshank

AMERICAN BIRDS
A Bantam Book / published by arrangement with The Ridge Press, Inc.

PRINTING HISTORY
Bantam edition / September 1978
2nd printing ....July 1974
3rd printing ....July 1976
4th printing ....September 1978
5th printing ....December 1980
6th printing ....April 1983

For information address: The Ridge Press, Inc. 25 West 43rd Street, New York, N.Y. 10036.

ISBN 0-553-23530-3
D. L. TO: 36 -1983
Library of Congress Catalog Card Number: 77-77600

Published simultaneously in the United States and Canada

Bantam Books are published by Bantam Books, Inc. Its trademark, consisting of the words "Bantam Books" and the portrayal of a rooster, is registered in the United States Patent Office and in other countries. Marca Registrada. Bantam Books, Inc., 666 Fifth Avenue, New York, New York 10103.

PRINTED IN SPAIN BY ARTES GRÁFICAS TOLEDO, S.A.

15 14 13 12 11 10 9 8 7 6

Contents
(with birds listed in official Check-List Order)

Why Study Birds?

The pastime of getting to know a variety of birds is called "birding," and the bird watchers who engage in it are numerous, enthusiastic, and at times fiercely competitive about the tallies of birds they have observed. There is excitement in building a good day's list, a big year's list, or an impressive "Life List" studded with rarities. For beginners, especially, the list is a spur to accomplishment. With practice — that is, after the several hundred species that may occupy a region have been learned — the beginning birder may have the fun of "breaking 100," sighting that many different species, in a single day.

But the list should not become the focus of birding, the way a score does to a golfer. Time spent in bird habitats should encourage awareness of the wonderful complexity of the earthly environment, of plants and soils and their relationship to the existence of all other things, of the effects of climate as demonstrated in the reproduction, migration, and daily life cycle of the birds. As knowledge grows, so will curiosity about such questions as why one species is rare and another common, or how small, warm-blooded animals withstand sub-zero cold or nonstop migration flights across oceans, or how the grebes are able to change specific gravity in order to submerge in the water.

A person's widening experience in the natural world should also sharpen his sense of responsibility for preserving it from despoliation. Observers soon learn that birds are delicate barometers of environment, flourishing or declining in response to the quality of their surroundings. From this awareness it is but a short step to helping ensure that all living organisms are permitted to exist healthfully and in balance. Conservation thus becomes a vital human enterprise.

Bird Groupings

The Contents (pages 3-5) list all the birds illustrated in this book in the order of their appearance in time—the oldest species first, the youngest last. This arrangement is based on our present knowledge of the fossil history of birds and on detailed studies of their evolution. It is called the "Check-List Order" by the American Ornithologists' Union, a professional society. The A.O.U. appoints a committee of experts to decide on the many questions involved in working out the family tree of the bird species. The latest edition of the official "Check-List of North American Birds" appeared in 1957. Between editions of this work, the Check-List Committee has the task of evaluating new information about the birds as it appears in various scientific journals. On the basis of this knowledge the committee may shift species from one group to another, or even change their names.

Classifying the birds — or any group of organisms — is difficult but fascinating work. It requires an understanding of the degree of relationship exhibited by populations of individuals. Relationship (in a changing, evolving population) is suggested not only by external appearances, but by details of internal anatomy, including bones, muscles, blood serum, egg proteins, and even behavior. This process of classification is called taxonomy, and it is an important branch of biology.

The basic unit of classification is the species, a population made up of similar individuals that occupy a common territory and interbreed. These individuals vary among themselves (since every living thing is unique), but their similarities exceed their differences. The test of a good species is successful interbreeding. Individuals of different species do occasionally interbreed, but their offspring are usually infertile.

For convenience in classification, two or more species that suggest a common origin are grouped together in a higher category called the Genus. Similar Genera are then grouped together into Families, and the related Families together form an Order, the highest, most inclusive, of the taxonomic groups.

The scientific names of birds and other living things always consist of at least two parts: a genus name (always capitalized) and a species name (capitalized only when it is based on the name of a person). Such a designation is called a binomial.

For example, the Robin's scientific name is *Túrdus migratórius. Túrdus* is a genus of typically chesty thrushes distributed around the world, but the species *migratórius* is that very characteristic North American population of red-breasted thrushes we in America call Robin. (There are other birds called Robin in various countries of the world, however.)

It is helpful to learn both the arrangement of Orders (because you can locate these groups quickly without having to go to the index in the bird book you are using), and the generic names of the birds you learn (first word of the binomial designation), since this will help you grasp the relationships between species.

Ornithologists currently recognize about 8,600 species of birds in the world. Only about 650 of these breed regularly in the United States and Canada. Only 120 species are illustrated in this "first book" of birds, but they are the ones most beginners across the country are likely to see and recognize in their first year or so of bird-watching. You cannot see all the birds mentioned in this book unless you travel, since some occur only in the East or in the West. But you can probably learn 50 birds in your own area in a short time.

Bird Names

Many common names of American birds date from the colonial period when the newly arrived settlers attached Old World designations to any birds that resembled familiar species of their homelands. The names, in most cases, were quite inaccurate, failing to distinguish birds according to their true ornithological relationships. But, since no one had yet studied or classified the birds of North America scientifically, no better names were available.

Because the popular and convenient names have persisted, however, contemporary nomenclature continues to be in a state of confusion. For example, the American Robin, except for its red breast, is totally unlike the European Robin. It is, in fact, more closely related to the European Blackbird. Our Blackbird, on the other hand, is a member of the typically American family of orioles. And our Meadowlark is not really a lark, although our Horned Lark is.

To make matters worse, the same bird may be called by several different common names. The Buzzard and the Turkey Vulture are the same bird. In the northern states the Ruffed Grouse is often called "partridge," while in the South "partridge" usually refers to the Bobwhite, a member of the quail family. Among warblers, one must separate the Yellowthroat and the Yellow-throated, which are different birds entirely.

There are many other such confusions. The common names may seem easier to remember, but they are very unreliable indicators of family relationships among the birds. That is why even the beginner will find it helpful to learn the Latin names as he goes along (accent marks are shown to aid pronunciation). The system is logical and orderly and is the best way to progress quickly toward an expert knowledge of the birds.

The Variety of Birds

The great variety of bird species is the result of "selective breeding," the evolutionary process of adaptation to environment. Adaptation does not happen with an individual of a species; the process evolves over a long period of time. It begins, however, with the occurrence, perhaps by accident, of some factor that is advantageous for survival. This is genetically "selected" for perpetuation and is reinforced throughout succeeding generations, simply because the individuals possessing it are more likely to leave offspring than those less favored.

Aquatic birds, for instance, are "specialists" in living on and off the water. The adaptations they have developed include body conformation that allows swift passage through the water, paddle feet, and — in some species — specialized bills or special buoyancy characteristics.

The response of species to environment works two ways. Species stemming from the same stock on the bird family tree, but inhabiting different environments, may develop an amazing diversity of forms. Among Perching Birds (Order Passeriformes), the meat-eating shrike is equipped with the predator's hooked bill, while the insect-eating warbler has a fine, slender bill. Or consider the range of sizes within the parrot family: from 3¾ to 39 inches.

Conversely, birds coming from diverse stocks often have produced remarkably similar types in the process of adapting to similar environments. For example, the Meadowlark, a member of the American oriole-blackbird family and an inhabitant of grasslands, has a look-alike from a different family in the grasslands of Africa. This is the Longclaw, a member of the wagtail family and quite unrelated to orioles.

Two kinds of behavior — territoriality and predation — are important in the balancing of bird populations.

Most song birds are territorial during the nesting season; that is, they will not allow others of their own kind within a particular zone they have staked out for themselves. A male who cannot establish a territory of his own will not attract a mate. On the other hand, a territorial bird cannot extend his domination beyond his boundaries or to the next generation. His young will have to compete for territories the next year, and only a few will be successful.

Predation occurring between populations also regulates animal numbers. It often is assumed that because predators subtract from a supply of birds the population must be diminished. But this is not necessarily so. Predation sets in motion events that compensate for losses. If predators had not taken the eggs of ground-nesting ducks for thousands of years, the ducks would all tend to nest at the same time, and thus could be wiped out by such catastrophes as prairie fires and hailstorms.

Predators and their prey have been living together for a long time and are therefore adapted to each other. The predator is not really an enemy.

Actually, we know very little about these subtle interactions in nature, and we are much too casual about tampering with them. We have introduced exotic species — the Starling, for example — without appreciating the possible danger to established native bird populations that may or may not be able to compete with the aggressive newcomers. The Purple Martin, the Bluebird, and the Red-headed Woodpecker are species that have almost certainly suffered declines because of competition from the Starling.

Change in environment — periods of drought or heavy rainfall, for example — can cause many populations to change drastically, some declining in number because living conditions are temporarily unsuitable, others profiting from the same changes.

The introduction of long-lived chemical poisons into the environment is one of the most drastic artificial changes ever to occur in nature. Only species with very large — and thus variable — populations and a short life span are able to adapt to such a change. But organisms with small populations and long lives cannot produce enough pre-adapted individuals quickly enough to maintain themselves in the contaminated environment, and so they perish.

For example, insects and small fish that become resistant to certain insecticides nevertheless absorb them, often in greater quantities than were required originally to kill the nonadapted members of the population. They therefore transmit a stronger dose of poison to those species that feed on them. Three or four such steps lead to a great concentration of poison, and the unlucky species at the end of the food chain — such as birds which have eaten fish which have eaten crustacea which have eaten plankton — may be seriously affected and in fact brought seriously close to extinction. The extent of the damage to nature is difficult to realize. Most people tend to look for declines in total bird populations, while discounting the loss of individual species as accidental.

For birders, the point is to realize that nature is not static, but dynamic, an equilibrium that works on an enormously large and complex scale. Birds are participants in the drama; and man, as friend and protector — or as blunderer — has his role to play, too.

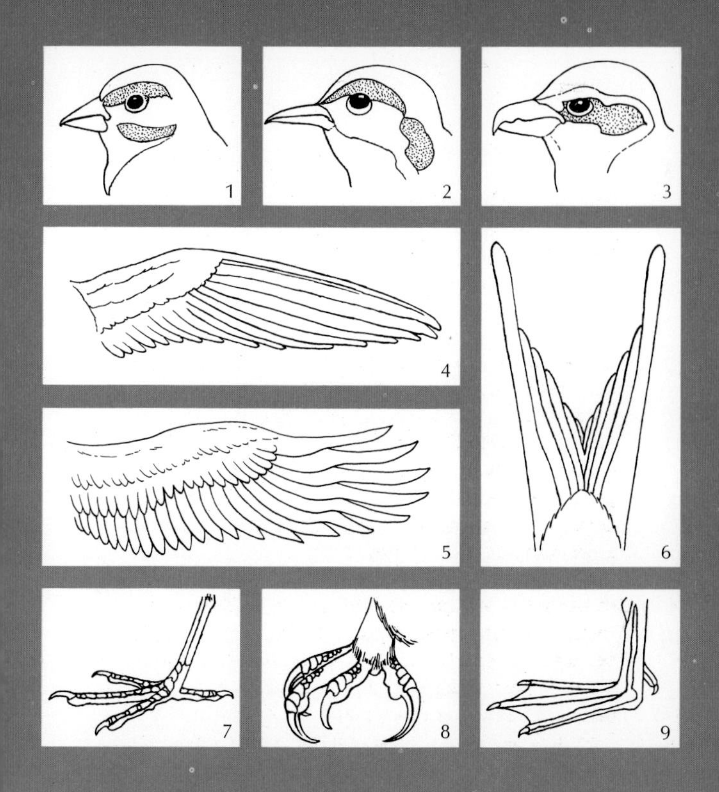

Adaptations

Through the process of natural selection, the bird species develop physical characteristics that enable them to compete successfully for survival. Several such adaptations are pictured above, and their functions are as follows. BILLS: (1) seed cracking, (2) insect eating, (3) flesh eating. WINGS: (4) swift flight and maneuverability, (5) soaring flight. TAIL: (6) extreme maneuverability. FEET: (7) perching, (8) preying, (9) swimming.

Guidelines to Bird-Watching

The expert usually spots his bird at a glance. Even if he can't identify the species or subspecies that he has in the field of his binoculars, he knows the group, usually even the genus, to which it belongs.

How does the expert do it? Actually, little thought is involved. Habit, training, and close acquaintance with birds enable the ornithologist to recognize a species when he sees it. However, in the process of recognition there is an orderly progression from general to specific characteristics. The expert follows this method almost subconsciously. The beginner who trains himself to think in terms of this progression will find that it speeds up his facility for making sure identifications.

It is not at all difficult to do. Only 18 Orders of birds are regularly represented in North America, and the characteristics of these Orders are easily remembered. To the expert they become second nature. Within an Order there may be one or more Families, each with its own differentiating set of characteristics that the observer can match against the bird under observation. After the bird is classed according to Family, the next step to identification is the Genus: body proportion and type of bill are the principal signposts here. Finally the expert decides the species of the bird in view, and even here he confirms his judgment with a second look at points of coloration and detail.

Of course, in any locality the range of possibilities is narrowed at the outset by the "local list" — the species that can be expected in a certain area at a certain time. This knowledge is doubly helpful: Details that do not match expectations alert the expert bird watcher to the possible presence of a rare or occasional species.

The scientific side of ornithology comes alive through actual observation. In the outdoors, one does not think in terms of Order, Family, Genus, and Species. The attention is focused on the living bird seen in the trees, in the air, on the ground. Unlike a museum specimen, it cannot be examined close-up and at leisure. If ever a picture was worth a thousand words it is now! For without a tutor to point out and name each species, the beginning birder needs the guidance of good pictures. (If you can memorize bird pictures beforehand at home, you are that much ahead of the game afield.) But in matching a picture to a bird in view, you must be thorough. If shape, proportion, and color match, check details of bill, legs, and tail.

The two usual approaches to bird illustration are drawings and photographs. The advantage of a drawing is that it allows a subtle emphasis to be put on "field marks," diagnostic details that immediately separate one species from others that may closely resemble it.

The photograph has its own advantages, especially when it shows a characteristic pose. The importance of "character" in birding can't be stressed too much. Of all the poses a bird may strike momentarily as it moves about, one is more typical than others, and once learned it will help you to recognize that species. A Robin's chestiness, especially on landing; a cuckoo's slinking trimness; the cut of a gull's wings — these are identifying characteristics to look for.

Another asset of photographs taken in the field is that they help the birder to associate a species with its proper habitat. Photographs in this book were chosen for their fidelity to the character of the birds discussed. In all cases we have focused on the male, but placed a female symbol (♀) where a female is shown.

Where to Look for Birds

Birds operate within a habitat, or home range. This is the necessary minimum of space required to meet their daily needs on a seasonal basis. Whether marsh, grassland, underbrush, or forest, the habitat must provide adequate food and water, and appropriate cover in which birds may nest and be protected against the elements and predators. Learning the characteristics of these habitats will provide the basic clues to the location of species, for the birds will seek the same environment wherever they are, year after year.

In spring, most small birds stake out a breeding territory within their habitat, and opportunities for observing them are at their greatest, for the birds are then very active and noisy.

The male's song in spring is his way of giving notice that he has established a territory and stands ready to defend it against interlopers of his own species. It is, then, an excellent means of locating species. Spring song is most intense during the hour or so after dawn and is repeated less intensely before dusk. It is irregular and infrequent at other times. When the young hatch (after an incubation period of from 12 to 24 days), the parents are busy finding food; ard when the young leave the nest, song is abandoned unless the parents go immediately into another nesting cycle. Otherwise the parents probably will molt their summer plumage, and in that case they become silent.

In seasonally cold or dry regions, birds must migrate in order to find the food they need to maintain body functions; thus many birds occupy different summer and winter ranges, or different dry-season and wet-season ranges. The geographical distribution of a species is the total area that the species occupies on a year-round basis.

The best way to approach birds is to move slowly and quietly. During the nesting season your leisurely movements at a discreet distance will allow you to observe the regular comings and goings of parent birds carrying food to the nest. Young birds in the nest often clamor for food, so an attentive ear can soon locate them. If, however, you approach a nest closely you may cause its destruction by other animals that may be watching you, or that follow your scent later out of curiosity.

After the nesting season many birds wander about as family groups, while the young are taught to fend for themselves. Remember that at this season there will usually be more young birds than adults, many of them difficult to identify because their plumage is a nondescript brown.

When fall migrations begin, many of these inexperienced young will be blown off their course, especially if the species is one that migrates at night. Since westerly winds predominate over much of the country in autumn, this means that southbound migrants will drift eastward. When they reach the Atlantic Coast they must stop or be lost at sea. As a result of this drift, the best place to find a variety of birds in autumn is on points of land that jut out to sea. Early morning is the best time, because after resting and feeding, the windblown migrants disperse and resume their southward movement.

In winter, look for birds in sheltered areas with ample plant cover, especially where food and water are also present. Time of day is less important now. Birds seek out the lee side of hills and other available protection from the wind that otherwise saps so much of their energy. These lee areas, if sunny, are several degrees warmer than open ground.

Life Zones of North America

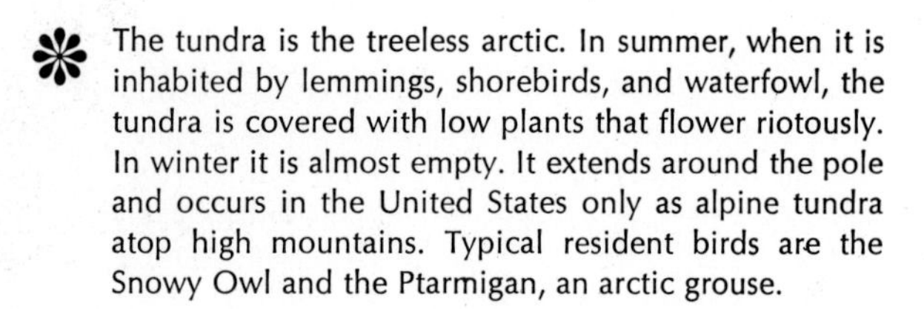

The tundra is the treeless arctic. In summer, when it is inhabited by lemmings, shorebirds, and waterfowl, the tundra is covered with low plants that flower riotously. In winter it is almost empty. It extends around the pole and occurs in the United States only as alpine tundra atop high mountains. Typical resident birds are the Snowy Owl and the Ptarmigan, an arctic grouse.

This is the northern and coniferous-forest zone that supports spruce, larch, and fir (softwood evergreens). There are few sharp lines between this and adjacent zones, but many transitional areas: open spruce-lichen woodland on the north, pineland on the south. Typical birds are the Goshawk and Red-breasted Nuthatch.

Grasslands grow where rainfall is less than 30 inches per year, usually in the center of continents, away from the oceans that normally provide moisture for rain and snow. Our eastern prairie is a tall-grass prairie; the western prairie has short grasses or bunch grasses. Grassland birds include the Meadowlark, Horned Lark, and Long-billed Curlew.

The eastern deciduous forest — the richest of its kind in the world — is a woodland of summer-green hardwoods. In the northern part grow beech, birch, and maple; in the central, mostly oak and hickory; and in the south, tulip, gum, and a great variety of smaller trees. Birds include the Blue Jay and Tufted Titmouse.

The tropics touch the continental United States only in south Florida and extreme south Texas. Palms, mahogany, and gumbo limbo are typical trees. Characteristic birds are sea birds, especially the Frigatebird.

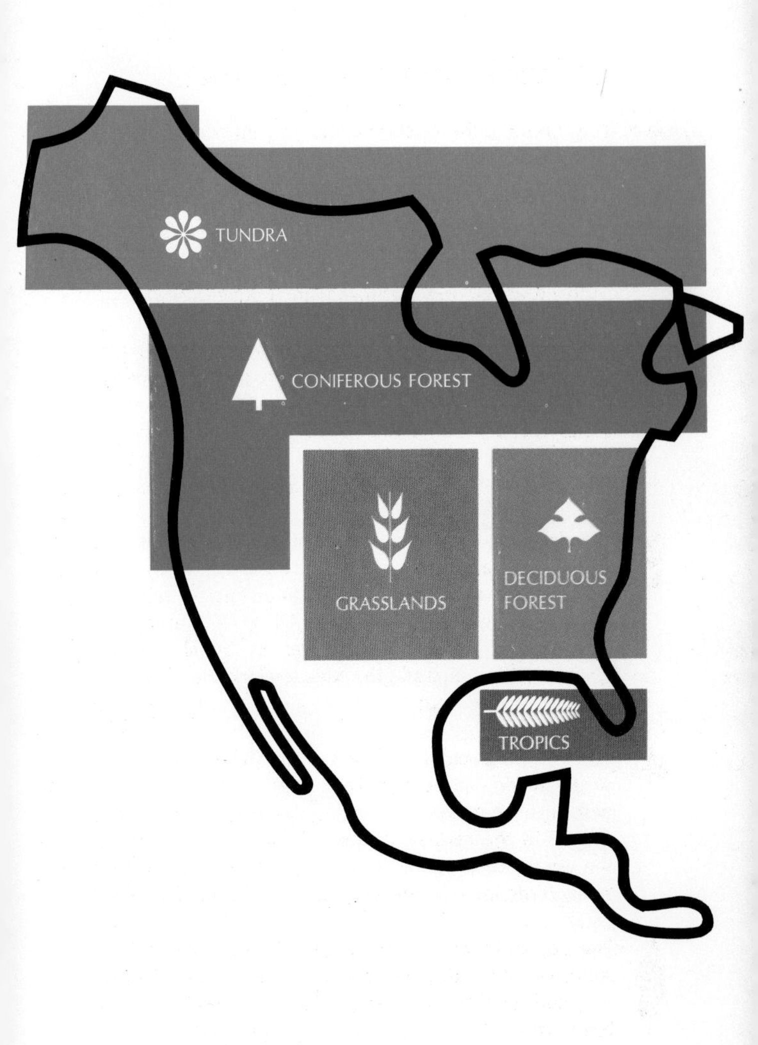
TUNDRA
CONIFEROUS FOREST
GRASSLANDS
DECIDUOUS
FOREST
TROPICS

Loons

Listed first because they are considered the oldest Order of American birds, the loons are large water birds with a short neck, heavy rounded head, and stout, pointed bill. They ride low on the water, are northern nesters, and winter along both coasts.

Common Loon

Gávia ímmer

This great northern diver is a lonely summer occupant of spruce-country lakes where its laughing call rings loudly and weirdly. Shown here is summer plumage; in winter, when the bird inhabits salt water, it is plain gray above, white below. As in other loons, the flight is strong, with neck and legs held low, giving a humpbacked appearance. The less numerous Red-throated Loon (*G. stelláta)* is slimmer, has a slightly upturned bill, and is red-throated in summer only. The Arctic Loon (*G. árctica)* looks like a small Common Loon and winters mostly on the Pacific Coast.

Grebes

These are the "Hell divers," smaller and shorter-bodied on the water than loons. They have an uncanny ability to vary specific gravity, sinking quietly like a submarine, without a ripple.

Western Grebe

Aechmóphorus occidentális

This is the largest and most striking of the grebes, of

medium size with a very long, slim, white neck and contrasting dark hindneck. The bill is thin and pointed. Breeding colonies occupy weedy western lakes. A fascinating courtship "dance" is performed in spring. The pair skitters along the surface with wings uplifted, necks bent, and bodies almost erect. Sizable flocks winter together, mostly on the Pacific Coast. The five other grebe species are smallish; they flock less, are more difficult to identify than the distinctive Western Grebe.

Pelicans, Cormorants, and Allies

The Pelecaniformes include six families of fish-eating birds scattered about the oceans of the world and in many inland lakes and large rivers. Being aquatic, they all have webbed feet. Most of them are colonial, sometimes nesting by the thousands on favored rocky islands where an abundant fish supply permits congestion without undue competition for food. This is especially so of Gannets, Boobies, and Cormorants, less so of Pelicans, Frigatebirds, and Tropicbirds.

White Pelican

Pelecánus erythrorhýnchos

One of our most spectacular birds, afloat or awing. It nests in tightly-packed island colonies in lakes west of the Mississippi, with one colony also on the south Texas coast; winters on southern coasts from California to Florida. It is social, flying in formation and feeding co-operatively in shallow water by forming a living seine. Its flapping flight is strong, but it never dives as the Brown Pelican of the ocean coasts does. Because of its size (9-foot wingspan), black wing-tips, and white body, it is sometimes confused with the Whooping Crane.

Brown Pelican

Pelecánus occidentális

Restricted to southern saltwater coasts, this big bird is especially familiar in Florida and California. A powerful flier, it alternates firm strokes with short glides, and often skims the waves, alone or in long lines. It dives into schools of fish for its food — an abrupt, water-splashing performance from as high as thirty feet in the air. These dives immerse it completely, but the bird always bounces up facing in a direction opposite to its entry. Occasional birds become very tame and then may take to begging clownishly for food at fishing piers.

Double-crested Cormorant

Phalacrócorax aurítus

Large, blackish (immatures are light-breasted) birds that nest in colonies on inland lakes or the Gulf and northern coasts, and winter on southern coasts. Called "shag," these are the famous, captive fishing birds of the Orient. They perch or sit erect, swim with uppointed bill, and fly with the whole body inclined upward. Their wingbeats are faster than those of geese, which they otherwise resemble, since they also fly in lines and V's. The four other species in the U.S. are not easily distinguished from each other. The Anhinga or Snakebird of southern swamps is a close relative.

Waterfowl

There are several groups of water birds, but only the ducks, geese, and swans are properly called waterfowl. The United States has forty-eight species, grouped in seven subfamilies but all of one family, the Anatidae. All have completely webbed feet. Most of them are vegetarians, but some feed on shellfish, insects, and even on fish.

Whistling Swan (preceding pages)

Ólor columbiánus

This big white bird nests on the Arctic tundra and migrates down the continent's interior to winter on both coasts, mostly off North Carolina and California. The even larger Trumpeter Swan (*O. buccinátor*) is a northwesterner, nesting from Yellowstone to southern Alaska. It is impossible to distinguish from a Whistling Swan on the wing. The Mute Swan *(Cýgnus ólor)* is a European bird which now nests in coastal ponds from New Jersey to Massachusetts. Our native swans give goose-like calls. Young swans are grayish-brown and even more difficult to differentiate than their parents.

Canada Goose

Bránta canadénsis

This is the commonest, best-known wild goose, usually a large, plump bird, brown and white with a black neck and white cheeks. Some regional populations (subspecies) are darker and no larger than Mallards, however. Flocks often form V's in flight, and honk loudly and sweetly. The smaller forms (mostly western) cackle rather than honk. Canadas feed in shallow water by "tipping," but also graze upland pastures a good deal. These are "weather migrants," pushing north as soon as the ice breaks in the spring, and southward when freezing weather crowds them out.

Snow Goose (right, with Blue Goose)
Chén hyperbórea

These lovely birds have black wing-tips like the White Pelican and Whooping Crane but are small compared to those two protected species. They nest on the Arctic tundra and migrate across a broad front, but they are less well known than the Canada Goose because of their generally uninterrupted flights — with stops in only a few favorite places unless forced down by weather — and their restricted Gulf Coast wintering grounds. There, however, they flock in large numbers. The similar, but darker Blue Goose *(C. caerulèscens)* is interbreeding and "swamping out" the Snow's white plumage.

Mallard

Ánas platyrhýnchos

This is *the* wild duck. It occurs nearly everywhere in Eurasia and North America, most abundantly in the prairies of the Mississippi valley. Drakes are easily told by their iridescent green head and chestnut breast; ducks (females) are a plain speckled brown, but have distinguishing white bars before and after the blue speculum patch of the wing. Like all surface-feeding (tip-up) pond ducks, they jump from the surface on take-off, and like the others, Wood Ducks excepted, they are ground-nesters. The familiar quacking is the female's call; males have a reedy note.

Black Duck

Ánas rúbripes

What the Mallard is to the interior, the Black is to the East Coast, though it is never so numerous. A dark brown bird with a paler head and neck and yellow bill (green in female), it has a flashing white underwing and reddish legs. Isolated pairs breed throughout the interior, prefer coastal ponds in winter, but use salt marshes and even saltwater bays when ice locks them out. The Mottled Duck *(A. fulvígula)* is a resident Gulf Coast species about halfway between a Black and a Mallard in appearance, like a dark female Mallard, but with dark tail and only one white wing-bar.

Pintail

Ánas acúta

Dapper, slender, trim, agile, swift — all these adjectives apply to the drake Pintail, which is further distinguished by a coffee-brown head, long white neck, a long pointed tail, and dark slender pointed wings. Among the most widely distributed of all ducks, it is also common to Eurasia. It is abundant in the West — crowding together in tight flocks in winter — and it occurs sooner or later wherever there are shallow, weed-filled ponds. The female is less distinctive but more slender, plainly marked, and longer-necked than the other mottled pond ducks she resembles.

Shoveler

Spátula clypeáta

A riotous version of the Mallard: green-headed but with a chestnut patch on the flanks; it shows a unique neck-to-tail waterline pattern of white-dark-white-dark. Its conspicuous spoon-shaped bill — for which hunters call it Spoonbill — and the chalk-blue shoulder-patches, seen best in low flight, are equally distinctive. The female, though she has the heavy, spatulate bill and blue shoulders, resembles the hen Mallard, as do so many of these ground-nesting females of the pond ducks, who must blend into their straw-colored nests to avoid disturbance.

Wood Duck

Aix spónsa

The gaudiest of North American pond ducks, although its colors are metallic and appear dark except in direct light. The dark wings and long black tail are distinctive in flight, as is also the high-pitched whistle. The drake often shows a crest. Females are best told by their tear-shaped white eye-ring; in late summer males in molt resemble females and young. These are birds of weedy ponds and streams in wooded regions; they are especially fond of acorns of the pin oak. They nest in hollow trees or in suitably large nesting boxes set out for them.

Scaup

Aýthya maríla, A. affínis

The two Scaups, Greater and Lesser, are common diving bay ducks that often crowd together in rafts of hundreds or thousands of birds. Black fore and aft, white below and gray above, the drakes have a metallic sheen to their black heads. The females are brown ducks with a white face. Both sexes have a blue bill, whence the sportsman's name, Bluebill. All have a white stripe along the trailing edge of the wing, which is longer in the Greater Scaup than in the Lesser. These two species are very difficult to tell apart in the field.

Common Goldeneye

Bucéphala clángula

This diving duck nests in hollow trees around northern spruce-country ponds, but is more often seen wintering in pairs or small groups on large lakes or bays, or on the ocean within a mile or so from shore. The drake's puffy black head may shine green and it has a diagnostic white facial spot. White on the waterline, the bird shows a white wing-patch in flight and its wings whistle loudly, hence the hunter's name, Whistler. Females and young are gray with a brown head; they may be difficult to identify until they fly and show their wing-patches.

Bufflehead

Bucéphala albéola

One of our daintiest ducks; small, strikingly black and white (the drake), agile (it takes off without pattering), and fast-flying. It is somewhat like a small Goldeneye, but the drake's white head-patch is larger and goes over the crown. The females are gray ducks with a small but diagnostic white cheek-patch. The wings of Bufflehead do not whistle in flight; and the birds feed in shallower waters than Goldeneyes. They nest in northwestern prairie parklands and winter on ice-free lakes and bays.

Ruddy Duck

Oxyúra jamaicénsis

A small diving duck that prefers weedy ponds but frequents bays and broad streams in winter. The white cheeks and the uptilted spike tail identify its chunky form in any plumage. No species is so surprising in its seasonal plumages: bright cinnamon in summer, plain brownish-gray in winter. Females are always gray and have a dark line across their white cheeks. All have short, dark wings and a fast, buzzing, somewhat erratic flight after a pattering take-off. Ruddy Ducks belong to a distinct, worldwide subfamily, the Stiff-tailed Ducks.

Common Merganser

Mérgus mergánser

Mergansers, or shelldrakes, are fish-eating ducks. Their bill is long and thin with tooth-like serrations to hold their slippery prey, which they actually can outswim. This is the largest, most cleanly-cut of the three merganser types. It is long on the water, white-bodied with a black back and blackish head that shines green in good light. It shows double white wing-patches in flight. Female is gray, with a reddish-brown head sharply demarked from its white breast. This is mostly a freshwater bird. Its flight has an arrowlike quality.

Raptors

The hawks, eagles, kites, vultures, and falcons are the daytime hunters whose predation helps stabilize the numbers of small animals. Even with their superior power, speed, and mobility, they are always scarce compared to their prey, as they reproduce more slowly; and to some extent their own numbers are controlled by the numbers of available prey. This interacting predator-prey relationship is typical of living systems in nature.

Bald Eagle

Haliaéetus leucocéphalus

This great bird, America's emblem, is no longer common but may still be seen in favored regions. Hundreds congregate to feed on fish at the tailgate of the large reservoirs on the lower Missouri and middle Mississippi rivers in winter. Others are scattered in extensive coastal estuaries where food is abundant and man is not a serious threat. Eagles resemble floating planks in the sky, because the white head and tail disappear against the blue. But the immature eagle is all brown (then resembling the Golden Eagle), and unfortunately is often shot for a "large hawk."

Turkey Vulture

Cathártes áura

Although related to birds of prey, this vulture's talons are too weak for predatory activity; it is instead a carrion-eating scavenger. The head is naked — red-skinned in the adult, otherwise gray. The bird aloft has a far more admirable appearance. Long-tailed, wings in a shallow V, banking from side to side, it soars to great heights in wide ascending circles, lifted on the thermal air currents that develop as the day grows warm. Vultures roost in groups, and early in the morning "hang" (spread) their wings to dry.

Red-tailed Hawk

Búteo jamaicénsis

Most widespread of the Buteos — fan-tailed, soaring, mouse-eating hawks — the Red-tail is still common, as hawks go. The adult's rusty-red tail is diagnostic, as is the wheezy call. Immatures are more difficult because their finely-banded, brownish tail is common to many Buteos, but, like their parents, they are husky in outline, heavy-shouldered when perched, and have a dark belly band. Red-tails prefer rough country, nest in woods, or even in tall cacti, and hunt rodents in open country. They often perch on phone poles and fence posts, where too many of them are shot.

Osprey

Pandíon haliáetus

This large, handsome hawk, once common on the Atlantic Coast and around large lakes, has decreased greatly since the 1950's due to poisoning of the hatchlings by chemical insecticides, such as DDT, which are transmitted from the mother's tissue to the eggs and through food. Unlike the Bald Eagle, for which many mistake it, the Osprey is white below, and its crooked wings have conspicuous black wrist-patches. It hovers over fish it spots from on high, and makes spectacular dives. The call is a shrill, repeated whistle. A great migrant, it is distributed almost worldwide.

Sparrow Hawk

Fálco sparvérius

Also called Kestrel, this is a spritely, colorful falcon hardly larger than a Robin. An open-country bird, it is still fairly common where fields provide its principal food — grasshoppers and field mice. Smallest of the hawk tribe, it has the typically pointed falcon wings and is a strong flier that hovers as it scouts for prey. It nests in old woodpecker holes, or even in nesting boxes, and has a shrill, often-repeated *killy* call. Both sexes are rusty brown above, but the male also has blue wings.

Gallinaceous Birds

This order of chicken-like birds includes the grouse, quail, turkeys, pheasants (the domestic chicken is a pheasant), and the Arctic-alpine ptarmigans. They are all stout-bodied, prefer running to flying, and have short, rounded wings that allow them to explode upward from a standing start. They eat grain and other seeds, fruit, and insects.

Bobwhite

Colínus virginiánus

This chunky, reddish-brown and white-faced game bird is more often heard than seen. Its delightfully extroverted three-note whistle, *bob-bob-white,* is familiar throughout the East almost everywhere old fields, brush areas, and open pine-lands occur in combination below the zone of heavy snow. Scattered in summer, Bobwhites in winter form sizable coveys and roost communally in a tight-packed circle, all birds pointing outward so that they can burst into flight if disturbed. Often called partridge in the South, a term sometimes used for Ruffed Grouse in the North.

California Quail

Lophórtyx califórnicus

This attractive bird is common on the Pacific Coast. Its curved, tear-drop head plume is always erect and very distinctive. It looks slate gray at a distance, travels in flocks, is very vocal, and prefers the brushy borders of oak woodland. The very similar Gambel's Quail *(L. gámbelii)* lacks the California's scale pattern on the belly (male has black patch) and·occupies the drier, semi-desert basins of the Southwest.

Ring-necked Pheasant

Phasiánus cólchicus

An Asiatic bird, now naturalized and common in many semi-open areas of the northern U. S., especially in corn and wheat country. It is a large stout bird unmistakable for its long, stiff tail. Hens are plain sandy brown; however, cocks are resplendent, with chestnut breast and iridescent head. Cocks often vary in details of markings because of the racially mixed stock involved in their propagation from game farms. The call is a raucous, two-note crowing, heard especially in the early morning in spring, when the polygamous cocks stake out territories.

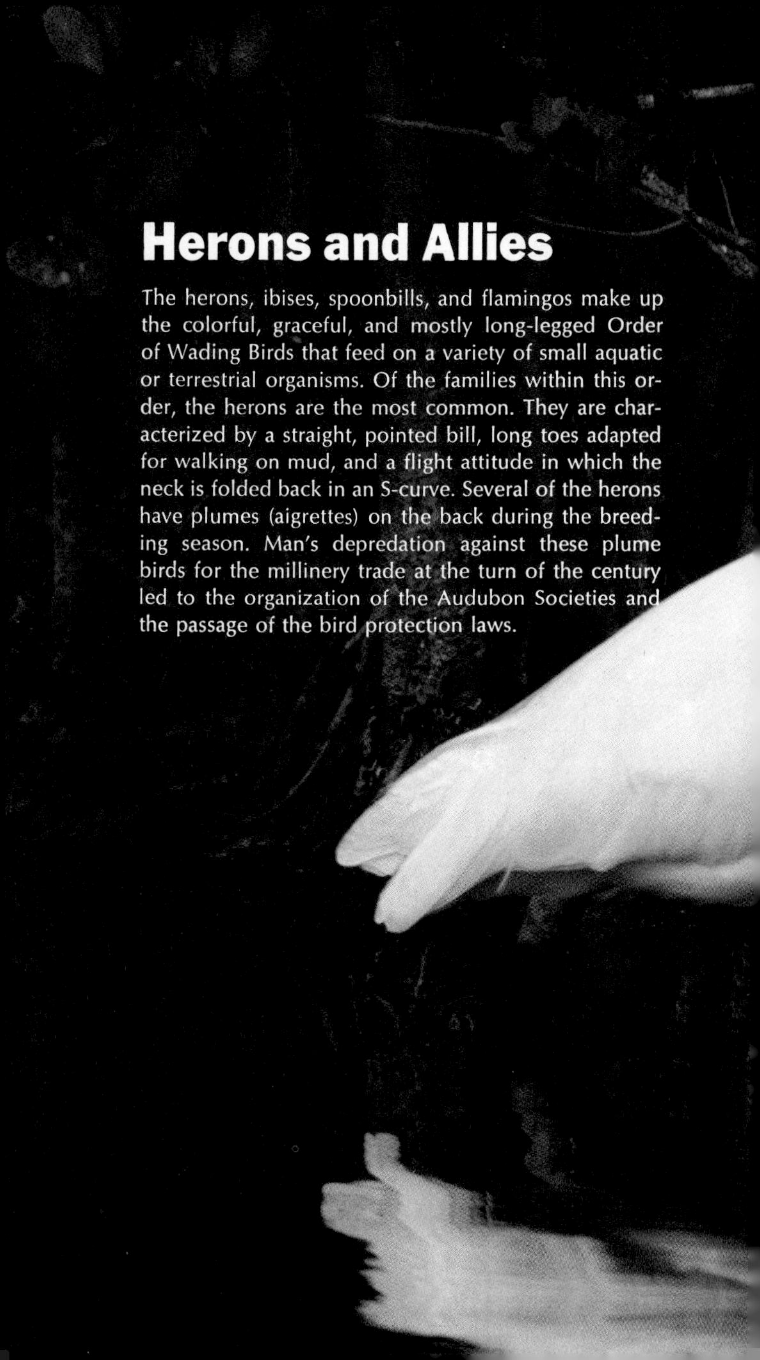

Herons and Allies

The herons, ibises, spoonbills, and flamingos make up the colorful, graceful, and mostly long-legged Order of Wading Birds that feed on a variety of small aquatic or terrestrial organisms. Of the families within this order, the herons are the most common. They are characterized by a straight, pointed bill, long toes adapted for walking on mud, and a flight attitude in which the neck is folded back in an S-curve. Several of the herons have plumes (aigrettes) on the back during the breeding season. Man's depredation against these plume birds for the millinery trade at the turn of the century led to the organization of the Audubon Societies and the passage of the bird protection laws.

Green Heron

Butorídes viréscens

A small, rather common, fast-flying heron which appears black at a distance, but blue-gray when close by in good light. The "green" responsible for its name is a gloss seen only in the hand or in exceptional light. Smaller than a crow, with a neck barely long enough to fold, the Green Heron is most easily recognized by its bright orange legs, chestnut breast, and bluish back, plus the loud, startling *squeouk* note it gives when surprised into sudden flight. It has several other notes, repeated *kucks* and *clucks*. It nests in loose colonies on fresh or saltwater shores.

Common Egret (preceding pages)

Casmeródius álbus

A large white heron of fresh and saltwater shores, with yellow bill and black legs. Other white herons are the larger Great White Heron *(Árdea occidentális),* with yellow legs, restricted to extreme south Florida. The smaller Snowy Egret *(Leucophóyx thúla)* has a dark bill and legs and bright yellow feet, hence the name Golden Slippers. The stocky, yellow-billed Cattle Egret *(Bubúlcus íbis)* is a recent immigrant from Africa and South America which feeds on insects in cow pastures of the eastern U. S.

Great Blue Heron

Árdea heródias

The tall, dark gray, more or less white-headed Blue Heron is often misnamed "crane," especially in the East where the paler, browner, true cranes (see p. 60) are rare. Unlike the crane, the Great Blue feeds in shallow water rather than in fields (although it sometimes hunts field mice in winter), and it draws back its head soon after take-off. It takes its prey with a lightning-quick thrust of the neck. When startled from its roosts or feeding grounds, it emits a series of gruff squawks. It is a colonial nester, either on Gulf Coast islands, or in swamps and bog borders farther north.

Black-crowned Night Heron

Nyctícorax nyctícorax

A stocky heron, with shorter neck and legs than most, and a thick bill. It feeds mostly at night, roosts in quiet woods in daytime, and nests in swamps in sizable, noisy colonies. Its comings and goings at dusk are punctuated by an unmistakable *quawk*. Adults are black above, white-bodied, and have a delicate white head-plume in spring, when the yellowish legs become almost orange. Immature birds are brown, speckled and streaked with white, and may be confused with the grayer immature Yellow-crowned Night Heron *(Nyctanássa violácea)*, whose adults are slate gray.

American Bittern

Botaúrus lentiginósus

This freshwater-marsh relative of the herons occurs across the continent but is easily overlooked because it "freezes" when frightened, bill to the sky, and looks like a dead stick among the cattails and reeds. Its "pumping" call, a guttural croaking, is unmistakable once it has been heard. Its streaky plumage is at first difficult to distinguish from that of immature Night Herons, but the bittern is more nearly mustard-brown and has black wing-tips. The half-size Least Bittern *(Ixobrýchus exílis)* is rarer (except in southern marshes) and has a black back.

Cranes, Rails, and Allies

Long-legged wading birds with a superficial similarity to herons, the Order of cranes, rails, coots, gallinules, etc. is of distinct lineage and quite diversified in size.

Certainly among the more striking of the group is the Whooping Crane *(Grús americána)*, a noble bird which has become the symbol of American wildlife conservation. With a narrow migratory range running down the middle of the continent—from the Wood Buffalo Park muskeg wilderness of northern Alberta, where it nests, to the Aransas National Wildlife Refuge near Rockport, Texas, where it winters—and a total wild population of only about fifty birds, the Whooper hardly deserves mention here except as the symbol that it is.

Sandhill Crane

Grús canadénsis

A tall, stately bird, the Sandhill Crane is slimmer, more uniformly colored and paler than the Great Blue Heron; adults appear pale in strong light, whereas young are brown (as pictured). These are prairie birds, occupants of freshwater sloughs in summer, rare in the East except in Florida and along the Gulf Coast. They flock in winter, and have a ringing, far-carrying, musical voice. Unlike herons, they fly with a quick upbeat and hold the neck straight out; they also soar a good deal.

American Coot

Fúlica americána

This common, duck-like bird with a china-white bill is related to the rails. Slate gray, with a black head and neck, it has a white patch under its stubby tail, rides buoyantly, and pumps its head as it swims. It dives for food, picks it from the surface, or filches it from ducks. When it climbs ashore, where it may also nibble plants, its strangely lobed toes (not webbed) are characteristic, as is its pattering take-off and weak flight with feet trailing. It nests on ponds throughout the West and winters on both coasts, usually in coastal ponds and in sizable flocks.

Shorebirds,

Gulls, and Allies

The sandpipers, plovers, and the gulls and terns, plus a few related forms, make up the large, diversified, and interesting order of Charadriiformes. The shorebirds (which strictly speaking include only the sandpipers and plovers) and some of the terns are the champion long-distance migrants among birds. Many nest on the Arctic tundra and winter on the grassy swales of the Argentine pampas, East Africa, or Australia; their incredibly long over-water flights are navigational feats.

American Avocet (preceding pages)

Recurviróstra americána

This is one of the showiest and most elegant of all shorebirds. Active, often noisy, it dashes about in shallows pursuing minnows and small invertebrates, and giving vent to a loud, sharp *wheet* cry. Avocets are taller than the other shorebirds they associate with. When sleeping — often on one leg — head and upcurved bill are tucked into the plumage of the back. They are fairly common on western ponds and sloughs, and gather in flocks on southern coastal ponds in winter. The pink-legged Black-necked Stilt *(Himántopus mexicánus)* is a close relative.

Killdeer

Charádrius vocíferus

Besides its plover characteristics — chunky body (compared to sandpiper relatives), pointed wings, and strong running gait — the Killdeer has a rather short, swollen bill. It is a pasture bird, and the most widespread nesting plover. It is also noisy *(killdee! killdee!)* and draws intruders from its eggs or young by dragging a wing to feign injury. It barely builds a nest, laying its eggs in a small, shallow scrape in a gravel patch, often in an old road rut in a field. As with all sandpipers and plovers, the young run about soon after hatching.

Spotted Sandpiper

Actítis maculária

A widely-distributed, fairly common but rather solitary sandpiper that summers by lakes and river margins, and winters along the southern U. S. coasts. It is spot-breasted only in summer, is otherwise clear-breasted and greenish-brown above. Its continual dipping — head down, tail up — and the shallow, stiff-winged flight, are unmistakable field marks. The call is a shrill, excited *peet-weet*. Its nest is most often in beach gravels, in the shade of a bush, from sea level to alpine ponds ten thousand feet above sea level in the Sierra Nevada and Rocky Mountains.

Long-billed Curlew

Numénius americánus

This largest of our sandpipers is a big, buffy bird of open grasslands, occurring from the Texas coast to the Canadian prairie and westward. Its down-curving bill is tremendously long, though the length varies greatly among individuals. In contrast to the smaller, more contrasty gray-brown Whimbrel *(N. phaéopus)* — a curlew of worldwide distribution — it is a uniform buff-brown except for cinnamon wing-linings that show in flight. Grasshoppers and the small crustaceans of the shore are its principal foods. It winters and migrates in flocks.

Lesser Yellowlegs

Tótanus flávipes

The two Yellowlegs, Greater *(T. melanoleúcus)* and Lesser, are common migrants wherever there are mud flats to provide the small wiggling animals on which they feed. These are the tall, brownish-gray shorebirds (waders) with long, bright yellow legs. Size is always deceptive in differentiating the two, except where direct comparison is possible, but the Greater Yellowlegs also has a longer, stouter bill which curves upward very slightly, and its call is a loud three-note whistle. The Lesser's bill is shorter, more slender, and its whistled call is softer and two-noted.

Great Black-backed Gull

Lárus marínus

Gulls are well-proportioned birds of the shore and inland waters, with gracefully tapered wings and deliberate flight. Web-footed, they swim easily, but they seldom dive, preferring to scavenge dead fish or flotsam, or take shellfish along shores, garbage at dumps, etc. The voice is a deep-throated *kow-kow-kow*. The Great Black-back is the world's largest gull, restricted to the North Atlantic and the Great Lakes in the U. S. A slightly smaller, dark gray, but otherwise similar Western Gull *(L. occidentális)* occupies the Pacific Coast.

Herring Gull

Lárus argentátus

The most widespread and abundant "sea gull," a white-bodied, silvery-backed water bird with black wing-tips, yellow bill, and pinkish legs. All young gulls are brownish for one to three years and thus somewhat difficult to distinguish. These are chocolate brown at first, then gradually grayer until adult plumage is acquired in fourth year. The West Coast's California Gull *(L. califórnicus)* is very similar, slightly smaller, with greenish-yellow legs. The Herring Gull is currently too numerous, feeding on man's superabundant floating garbage.

Laughing Gull

Lárus atricílla

A medium-sized, slate-backed gull of southern coasts (north to Maine in the East), black-headed in summer, with a loud "laughing" call. The very similar Franklin's Gull *(L. pipíxcan)* — with more white in the wing-tips — is a prairie bird, following the plow or taking insects, etc., in the air or in water. Immatures of both species are brown, with a white, black-tipped tail, and have a distinctive mewing call during their first summer. Since all black-headed gulls lose most of the black in late summer, rely then for identification on pattern and size.

Forster's Tern

Stérna fórsteri

Terns are slender, graceful, mostly white "sea swallows" with pointed bills and black caps (summer). The Forster's Tern migrates right across the U. S., nests on the Canadian prairie, and winters on all southern coasts, though it prefers marshes to beaches. Distinguish it from the Common Tern *(S. hirúndo)* — which is more common in the East — by the shiny white "wrist" (base of the long flight feathers) and by the black ear-patch in late summer when the black cap disappears. Common Tern has a raspy, drawn-out call, *kee-urrr;* Forster's is a flat *zrappp.*

Black Skimmer

Rýnchops nígra

This bird, a black-and-white relative of the terns and gulls, is distinctive for its water-skimming flight. Restricted to East and Gulf Coast bays, where it flocks on sand bars, its fishing methods are fascinating to watch. It often draws minnows to the surface of shallow waters by ploughing a thin furrow in the water with the lower mandible of its long, red, scissor-bill, then returns to snap up the curious fish that have investigated the disturbance. The Skimmer's bill is unique in that the lower mandible is longer by far than the upper.

Pigeons and Doves

Doves and pigeons are small-headed, short-legged birds that coo and bob their heads while walking, and fly swiftly and strongly. The term pigeon is usually applied to the stouter, fan-tailed members of the group, while dove refers to the slimmer, longer-tailed species; but neither "dove" nor "pigeon" is a diagnostic term. This is a worldwide order (Columbiformes) with many species, only a few of which occur in the United States.

Mourning Dove

Zenaidúra macroúra

This is the common wild dove of the U.S. and Canada, a fawn-brown bird with pointed wings and a long tapered tail that has white margins. The wings whistle in flight and the bird's name refers to the mournful quality of the call. It is considerably smaller than the once fabulously numerous Passenger Pigeon that darkened the skies of colonial America but is now extinct. Except in the North, this dove is our most hunted game bird.

Cuckoos

These slender, long-tailed birds of woodland and brush areas include several forest cuckoos — among them the European Cuckoo that gave the cuckoo clock its name; the black Ani of crossword puzzle fame; and the big Roadrunner of the Southwest, which is a ground cuckoo.

Yellow-billed Cuckoo (preceding pages)

Coccýzus americánus

Our most widely distributed cuckoo in summer, commonest where the tent caterpillar is abundant. It slips through the trees quietly, but its graceful form, the white tips of the tail-feathers, and the rufous wings are distinctive. The calls of the Yellow-bill, and the plainer Black-billed Cuckoo *(C. erythropthálmus)* of eastern North America, are less rhythmic than those of their cuckoo-clock cousin.

Roadrunner

Geocóccyx californiánus

The scientific name for this rugged, long-tailed, crested bird is truly descriptive, since it means ground cuckoo. This is a bird of mesquite and cactus country in the arid Southwest, and is most often seen by the side of the road, or taking off into the shrubbery, its tail trailing. An agile acrobat, it catches and eats snakes and lizards and such lesser fare as insects and occasional birds' eggs. Its song is a series of dove-like notes, on a descending scale.

Owls

Owls are Nature's nighttime predators, performing at night or during the hours of dusk the same role that hawks and their relatives perform during the day. They help to control the population numbers of smaller animal species, and to cull weak and sickly individuals. They are short-necked, large-headed birds, able to turn their heads almost all the way around; they have extremely keen hearing and are silent fliers.

Screech Owl

Ótus ásio

This small tufted owl occurs throughout the U.S. and southern Canada and is usually first identified by its soft, quavering whistle — either all on one key, or in a descending scale. It is a bird of small woodlots, suburbs, small farms, where it nests in hollow trees, or sometimes in a nesting box put out for flickers or Wood Ducks. It has two distinct color phases, gray and rusty, and some broods may contain owls of both types. Easy to recognize in the East, where it is the only small tufted owl, it has relatives in the West that are much less easily differentiated.

Great Horned Owl

Búbo virginiánus

This big, husky owl is the tiger of the woods, twice the size of the crows that invariably harry it when they discover its daytime perch in a pine or spruce tree. It is also the most widely distributed of the owls, nesting from the near side of the Arctic to the tip of South America. It has conspicuous ear tufts and is barred (crossways) on the belly rather than streaked. Its six or so notes are deep-throated and guttural, the *basso profundo* of the woodland. Despite its size and power — it can take skunks, crows, etc. — its food consists mostly of mice.

Barn Owl

Tyto álba

This pale, buffy, monkey-faced owl is responsible for many a story of haunted houses. It roosts in belfries, abandoned houses, barns, hollow trees, crevices in cliffs or banks. And, unlike the other owls, which take wing at dusk and occasionally during the day, it is strictly nocturnal. It appears white in the glare of automobile headlights. The call is a wheezy sneeze, most unlike other owls. It is among the farmer's best friends, since it is a living mousetrap. Despite this, it is too often shot.

Goatsuckers

These are strange insect-eating birds, soft-plumaged, large-eyed, large-mouthed, mostly nocturnal, and erroneously named for the old farmer's belief that they relieved goats of their milk. The group includes the Whip-poor-will, Poor-will, Chuck-will's-widow, and Pauraque, all related species named for their call. Except for the Nighthawk, these birds are commonly heard in early summer but are seldom seen except when the headlights of an automobile pick out their red eyes and flitting forms at night in country settings.

Common Nighthawk

Chordeíles mínor

These loud and raspy-voiced erratic fliers come out just before dusk in cities and towns across America; their nests often are on the gravel roofs of downtown buildings. Their wings — long, slender, and pointed — show a white patch at the wrist. Tremendous migrations of these birds move south in August and September.

Swifts and Hummingbirds

The name of this Order, Apodiformes, means "without feet," not quite descriptive, but a reference to the tiny feet of both these bird families. Neither ever walks on them; they use them only for perching. Swifts are aerial insect-feeders; they are fast-flying birds with stiff wings. The Chimney Swift *(Chaetúra pelágica)*—not to be confused with swallows — is a sooty-brown "flying cigar," the swift of the East. The West has the similar but slightly smaller Vaux's Swift *(C. vaúxi)* and the dashing White-throated Swift *(Aeronaútes saxátalis)*.

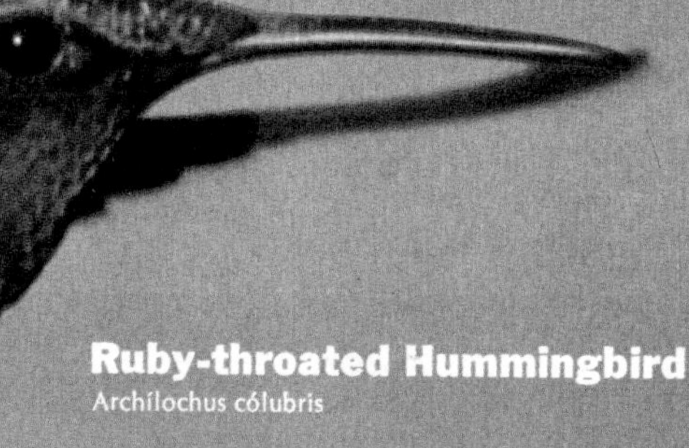

Ruby-throated Hummingbird

Archílochus cólubris

This tiny bird, the only one of its kind that nests east of the Rocky Mountains, makes an amazingly long migration hop across the Gulf of Mexico: 500 miles nonstop! Male hummers have a flashing iridescent throat or gorget — which, however, appears black except in directly reflecting light. Being nectar-feeders, these birds have long, slender bills and long, lapping tongues. Except for the male's gorget, the sexes are much alike: green above and white below, though females and young of both sexes have white-tipped tails.

Kingfishers

The stout, large-headed, colorful, and rather noisy kingfishers are a widespread family, though only one species occurs regularly in the U.S.

Belted Kingfisher

Megacéryle álcyon

A fairly typical kingfisher, though larger than most. It has weak feet, and walks only to enter or leave its nest burrow, cut into a steep bank near water. Its stout, pointed bill is a good pincer for catching small fish and crayfish. It often hovers on vibrating wings before diving head first into the water. The Kingfisher's loud, rattling call enlivens the water's edge. Both sexes are crested, both have a blue chest band, but the female also has a rusty belly band. When not flying, the Kingfisher sits quietly in a hunched-over position, its large head and bill often seeming about to overbalance it.

Woodpeckers

Woodpeckers are well equipped with a strong, chisel-like bill for drilling into tree trunks, both to gather wood-boring insects as food, and to build nest holes and roosting cavities for use in cold weather. They sit upright against the tree while pecking, propped by a stiff tail. On the wing they flap and glide and so have an undulating flight.

Pileated Woodpecker

Dryócopus pileátus

Uncommon but widely distributed in hardwood timber or mixed mature woodland, this is a crow-sized, black, startlingly red-crested woodpecker with white wing-linings. The exceedingly rare Ivory-billed Woodpecker *(Campéphilus principális)* of the Southeast from South Carolina to east Texas resembles it, but shows much more white in the wing, both at rest and in flight. The Pileated calls loudly, like a Flicker; the Ivory-bill has a thin, Nuthatch-like call.

Flicker

Coláptes aurátus, C. cáfer

This brown-backed, loud-voiced woodpecker is as much at home on the ground — where it eats ants — as in trees. As it flies away, its white rump is diagnostic, as also the underwing-lining, yellow in the Yellow-shafted Flicker of the East and North, but red in the western Red-shafted Flicker (*C. cáfer,* shown here). The facial color patterns of the two are interestingly reversed. Flickers drill three-inch diameter holes and a roomy nesting cavity, usually in dead trees. The most vocal woodpecker, it likes an exposed perch when giving its series of loud, often raspy *wicka-wicka* cries.

Downy and Hairy Woodpeckers

Dendrócopos pubéscens, D. villósus

White-backed, black-and-white barred, these are the common small woodpeckers that come to winter feeding stations across the country, especially where suet or peanut butter are added to the sunflower-seed mixture. Both males have a red patch on the back of the head. Although you may learn to distinguish them by call (Hairy's louder, harsher) and even by their tapping, the surest way is to notice the size of the bill: as long as the head in the Hairy, much smaller in the Downy. The Hairy nests in mature deciduous woodland, the Downy in orchards and other semi-open areas.

Downy Woodpecker

Perching Birds

This largest Order of birds includes 25 American bird families, the Passerines. All but the first, the Flycatchers, are members of the Suborder of Songbirds, even though some, like Crows, are hardly songbirds in practice, however well qualified otherwise.

The birds in the numerous family of Flycatchers are rather large-headed, raspy-voiced, and have such short legs that they perch erect and almost never walk. They launch forth to take insects in the air and their hunting circuits soon become almost predictable.

Western Kingbird (preceding pages)

Tyránnus verticális

Although its range overlaps that of the Eastern Kingbird in the plains and mountains, this is a truly western bird, occupying small clumps of trees around farms, in river bottoms, etc. It is less aggressive and harsh-voiced than the Eastern Kingbird, its colors are softer, with a wash of yellow below, a blended white throat, and white outer tail-feathers. The very similar Cassin's Kingbird *(Tyránnus vocíferans)* of the Southwest is a slightly chestier bird with a well-defined white throat but without the white outer tail-feathers.

Eastern Kingbird

Tyránnus tyránnus

Called "little chief" by the American Indians, this is a jealous guardian of its semi-open country territory against passing crows, hawks, etc., which it drives off angrily by diving from above. It is gray above, white below, and the conspicuous white band on the end of its black tail is diagnostic.

Great Crested Flycatcher

Myiárchus crinítus

This bird is representative of another large group of flycatchers — the genus *Myiárchus* — characterized by a puffy gray head, yellow belly, a long, bright rusty tail, and white wing-bars. This is a bird of mixed woodlands or woods borders. It nests in cavities and can be attracted to nesting boxes placed about ten feet off the ground at the edge of a patch of woods. Its loud, rather harshly whistled *wheep* call is distinctive. Although the only one of its group in the eastern U.S., it has several relatives in the Southwest, most of them difficult to distinguish from one another.

Eastern Phoebe

Sayórnis phoébe

This small, grayish, dark-headed bird — known as a fly-catcher by its erect posture and aerial sallies after insects — has the distinctive habit of flipping its longish tail downward with a leisurely, sometimes almost regular rhythm. Other small flycatchers have wing-bars; the Phoebe does not, except in the immature plumage of the first summer. Its *fee-bee* call, "spoken" not whistled, is unmistakable. Phoebes like to be near water and will nest under bridges, on summer camp porches, etc. Rely on voice in coming to know the highly similar small flycatchers.

Say's Phoebe

Sayórnis sáya

A typical Phoebe but unstreaked brown rather than gray, with warm rusty color on the belly and the under-tail coverts. As a westerner, it has learned to occupy the dry and sunny vicinity of ranches on the high plains, and the feet of bluffs and cliffs farther west. Its call is a slurred *chur-weer*. The Black Phoebe *(S. nígricans)* occupies the southwestern part of the same range, but prefers stream courses and their wooded rims. Junco-like in its black-and-white pattern, it is, however, a typical Phoebe in behavior, so there is no excuse for confusion.

Horned Lark

Eremóphila alpéstris

Unlike the Meadowlark, which is an oriole-blackbird relative, this is a true lark, and our own counterpart of the English Skylark. These are slender, brownish birds that *walk* (unlike sparrows, which hop); they have a black necklace, a yellow face, and white outer tail-feathers. Common in short-grass areas, we know them best in winter flocks, running about, lifting into the wind, and settling again. Males sing on the wing high above their nesting areas in pastures, golf courses, or on arctic-alpine tundra.

Barn Swallow

Hirúndo rústica

This most dashing, graceful, and colorful of our swallows is the only one of its tribe with a deeply-forked tail, and this is enough to identify it. It is dark steel-blue above and bright rust below. It builds a mud nest on a rafter inside barns or garages that are adjacent to large, open fields, especially if a pond or slough is present to augment the insect populations upon which it feeds while on the wing. Interestingly, this bird has almost forsaken natural nesting sites for man's buildings. Like all swallows, it spends most of its time awing or perched.

Cliff Swallow

Petrochélidon pyrrhonóta

This is the "swallow of Capistrano" and just as punctual in its spring return in your region as it is said to be in California. Although it is remarkably regular in its migrations, its comings and goings actually are not so clock-like as the legend would have it. It is chunkier than the more common Barn Swallow, square-tailed, with orange rump, and pale buff forehead. It builds a distinctive gourd-shaped nest of mud pellets under the eaves of barns near good pasturage, in groups varying from a few pairs to as many as a hundred pairs.

Tree Swallow

Iridoprócne bícolor

The commonest, most widespread swallow, greenish-blue above and pure white below. It nests in hollow trees or nesting boxes, especially near water. Along the Atlantic Coast and on the prairies it gathers in large fall migration flocks, often lining telephone wires shoulder-to-shoulder for hundreds of feet. In the West, the somewhat similar Violet-green Swallow *(Tachycinéta thalassína)* is distinguished by a white eye-patch and white flank-patches; don't confuse it with the White-throated Swift, which also has white flank-patches.

Purple Martin

Prógne súbis

The largest of our swallows, the male is a solid blue-black, the female and young brownish-gray. Broad wings allow the Martin to soar a good deal, and its liquid chatter and colonial habits (in multicelled boxes, or gourds in the South) make it a countrywide favorite. Although it feeds wholly on insects caught on the wing, its mosquito-eating function has been exaggerated; these swallows deserve a welcome for their own sake. Martins seem particularly susceptible to late spring storms that kill early insects; numbers of them succumb to cold and starvation.

Blue Jay

Cyanocítta cristáta

This common, colorful, and noisy bird is easily recognized but often unfairly accused of rascality. As is true of hawks and owls that occasionally take birds, the effects of the jay's backyard depredations are shown by objective study to be minor and easily repaired. The Blue Jay is especially common in oak woodlands, because acorns are a staple food. It is a conspicuous autumn migrant, flying in loose flocks at or just above tree-top height. However, not all jays migrate; except at the very northern limits of the range, many individuals stay on to winter in their usual habitats.

Steller's Jay

Cyanocítta stélleri

The dark, conspicuously crested, curious, and noisy jay of the West, especially in the somewhat open coniferous woodlands of middle altitudes, where Ponderosa Pine is dominant. There are two other common jays in the West, the Scrub Jay *(Aphelócoma coeruléscens)* and the Pinyon Jay *(Gymnorhínus cyanocéphalus)*, but only Steller's is crested. Like the Blue Jay of the East, Steller's Jay is expert at imitating hawks, especially the scream of the Red-shouldered Hawk. It is also our largest jay.

Black-billed Magpie

Píca píca

Striking in appearance, with a long, iridescent green tail, this crow-relative ranges over the West's open country — almost wherever the brush is dense enough to hide its bulky nest. A gregarious bird, it is usually seen in small, noisy flocks. It feeds on almost anything edible — including fruit, grain, carrion, mice, small snakes, eggs, even nestling birds. On occasion, Magpies peck at sores on the backs of range animals, for which ranchers object to them. Some of the oak-savanna valleys of central California's coastal ranges have Yellow-billed Magpies *(Píca núttalli)*.

Common Crow

Córvus brachyrhýnchos

These large, all-black birds with the flapping flight and noisy *caw-caw* cry are known to almost everyone. They flock a good deal, form sizable winter roosts, and like open fields and shores for feeding — which they do with a sentinel on guard. Although occasionally troublesome, these birds have been killed in excessive numbers over the years: as pests by farmers, as "varmints" by sportsmen. Fortunately, they have so far proved more clever than their persecutors. The Atlantic Coast also has a slightly smaller Fish Crow *(C. ossífragus)* with a flatter, more nasal voice.

Black-capped Chickadee

Párus atricapíllus

This pert, much-admired small visitor to winter feeding stations is common throughout the north temperate zone. Its much-overlooked song is a clear, high, two- or three-note, whistled *sweet-ie*. It nests in holes excavated in punky dead trees in young woodland. Most of the deciduous forest from New Jersey southward is occupied by the very similar, nonmigratory Carolina Chickadee *(P. carolinénsis),* a plainer bird with a higher-pitched song. In the entire Southeast, therefore, summer birds are Carolinas; but *winter* birds between New Jersey and Virginia may be either species.

Tufted Titmouse

Párus bícolor

This chickadee relative is distinguished by its crest; it also is somewhat larger, white-throated rather than black-bibbed, and a plainer gray; but it has the same rufous flanks and its voice has a number of husky, chickadee-like notes. It is common in good deciduous woodland, especially near streams; it flocks with chickadees in winter and shares their fondness for sunflower seed at feeding stations. The song is a distinctive, insistent *peta-peta-peta.* There are three other titmouse species in the Southwest.

White-breasted Nuthatch

Sítta carolinénsis

An acrobatic, "upside-down" bird with a blue-gray back, clean-cut black cap, white cheeks, and a pointed, slightly upturned bill. It gleans insects and insect eggs from the bark of trees, moving up or down — head first — with equal ease; but, like its chickadee and titmouse relatives, it is also fond of sunflower seed, peanut butter, and suet. The call is a snappy *yank-yank;* the song is a run-together *who-who-who-who-who.* Unlike our other nuthatches, which dwell among evergreens, the White-breasted prefers deciduous woodland, nesting in mature stands.

House Wren

Troglódytes aédon

This small, plump, brownish bird with the bubbling song is our commonest, most widely distributed wren, occurring where tall tangles of shady brush provide the cover these birds like, especially in the East. It is restless and pugnacious, driving off most other birds from the vicinity of its nesting boxes or crevices. Males build many false nests. The sharply cocked tail spells "wren," and there are several other species in the Southwest. The House Wren is more sparsely distributed in the West, and must therefore be distinguished from Bewick's Wren.

Bewick's Wren

Thryómanes béwickii

What the House Wren is to the North and East, this bird is to the South and the West. It is about the same size, but white below, with a conspicuous white eye-stripe, and a slightly longer, rounded tail bordered with white. The larger Carolina Wren *(Thryóthorus ludoviciánus)* of the East also has an eye-stripe, but it is buffy below and has a very different song. The Bewick's song is more wiry in quality than the House Wren's, thus less "bubbly" in character. All wrens scold a good deal and, being curious, can be attracted by squeaking, shushing, and such noises.

Mockingbird

Mímus polyglóttos

Like the tilted wings of the Turkey Vulture, the song of the Mockingbird is a better "indicator" of the South than the Mason-Dixon line. Day and night the Mockingbirds sing, and the country they occupy is the richer for it. It is a long-tailed, gray bird with large white wing-patches and white outer tail-feathers, and it perches conspicuously. Its slow wingbeats help to separate it from another southern bird, the Shrike. A great mimic of other birds' songs, it has a varied repertoire of musical phrases, each repeated several times.

Catbird

Dumetélla carolinénsis

This smaller, slate-gray relative of the Mockingbird prefers humid, shady tangles of deciduous trees and shrubs wherever these occur, except in the extreme Southeast and the Far West. The black cap and the rusty undertail coverts will confirm its identity, but perhaps best of all is the cat-like mewing that intersperses this bird's somewhat discordant song of single phrases. A poor imitator, and a much less versatile singer (compared to Thrashers or Mockers), the tail-flicking Catbird is a pleasant neighbor nonetheless.

Brown Thrasher

Toxóstoma rúfum

A common, dashing inhabitant of sunny openings in the borders or tall brush of eastern woodlands. Its bright rusty plumage and streaked breast suggest a thrush to many who misname it "Brown Thrush," but the long thrasher tail is diagnostic, as is the pale eye. Technically, with the Mockingbird and Catbird, it is a member of the Mimic Thrush family, but it is not truly a mimic. The song is rich in quality, with most of its phrases twice-repeated, and usually given from a conspicuous perch. There are several other thrashers in the West; their plumage is unstreaked and grayish.

Robin

Túrdus migratórius

A robust, chesty, typical thrush which is, however, only distantly related to its European namesake. Our Robin blankets North America during the nesting season and is thus America's best-known and perhaps its best-loved bird. Its cheery carolling, *cheeri-up, cheeri-up,* is a chief harbinger of spring for many of us. The long controversy over the headcocking posture of Robins when they feed on the lawn — whether to see, hear, or smell — has finally been resolved. The birds see worms sticking out of their holes in the ground. Young birds have a speckled breast.

Wood Thrush

Hylocíchla mustelína

America is fortunate in having five musical woodland thrushes. Handsomest of these, though not at all untypical, is the Wood Thrush. It is the easiest to learn because it stays on in the second-growth saplings of our ever-spreading suburbs. Notice the reddish head (Hermit Thrush has reddish tail), and the numerous large spots on the breast. A superior singer, its song consists of rich, flute-like phrases that are given a guttural twist. The other woodland thrushes are more of an identification challenge.

Eastern Bluebird

Siália síalis

Blue above and red-breasted, this soft-voiced, rather dumpy little thrush vies with the Robin for first rank as America's favorite small bird. The blue of its back is not a pigment, but a refracted color, so it appears dark when the light is not reflected directly. You will overlook many Bluebirds along roads in open country until you learn to identify their slightly hunched over posture and melodious voice. From the Rockies westward, another species, the Western Bluebird *(S. mexicána),* can be distinguished by its blue throat and rusty shoulders (male).

Mountain Bluebird

Siália currucoídes

A fairly common bird of the West's high country, especially above 5,000 feet in summer. Unlike the Eastern and Western Bluebirds, this bird lacks rusty breast coloring. The male is sky blue all over, the female gray and blue. This species also stands more erect when perched — rather than sitting hunched up; and it hovers more in pursuit of insects. These characteristics help make it more conspicuous and a quite delightful bird for those lucky enough to enjoy it.

Cedar Waxwing

Bombycílla cedrórum

This is a small, crested bird with elegant pinkish-brown plumage. The yellow tip of its tail, and the thin, high, single note, are easy clues to identity; but the little red "wax" tips of the wings that give the bird its name require a close look. This is a fruit-eater (mountain ash, cherry, etc.), a great wanderer, and as much at home catching insects on the wing as eating cherries. When wild cherries become overripe and winy, the Waxwings may sometimes be seen lining telephone wires, leaning on each other, obviously drunk.

Loggerhead Shrike

Lánius ludoviciánus

Shrikes are predators that nature has evolved from among the songbirds themselves. Though they do take some small birds, their principal food is large insects and mice, and what seeming "damage" they do is easily absorbed and made up by their prey populations. A gray, white, and black bird, superficially like a Mockingbird, it is often overlooked. Notice the black brow line, the hooked bill, and the quick wingbeats. Every few years, in winter, the larger-billed Northern Shrike *(L. excúbitor)*, especially its brownish young, visits the northern U.S. from subarctic Canada.

Starling

Stúrnus vulgáris

An introduced, naturalized Old World bird that has colonized the continent aggressively and is often a nuisance because in winter it flocks and roosts by the thousands in cities. The Starling looks like a glossy, short-tailed blackbird, though it belongs to a different family. It has a yellow bill in spring and summer. The young are brown, the winter birds speckled. Unfortunately, Starlings also compete with native birds for nesting cavities, and tend to dominate winter feeding stations when they gather in groups, though single birds are not at all aggressive.

Yellow Warbler

Dendroíca petéchia

The American Wood Warblers are a large, colorful, and varied family of birds that test the watcher's skills because they seldom sit still for examination. The Yellow is the most widespread of all our warblers, a small, all-yellow, fine-billed bird. It is less a bird of woodland than of shrubbery such as mangrove, alders, willows, or even orchards. The male has red streaks on its breast; and regardless of sex or age, the tail is tipped with yellow spots. It is not an open-country bird like the Goldfinch (page 148).

Myrtle Warbler

Dendroíca coronáta

An abundant bluish-gray warbler, with yellow rump, yellow shoulder-patches, and white throat. It nests in northern spruce country, migrates right across the U.S., and winters in numbers farther north than other warblers, often feeding on insects in the windrows of kelp on beaches, or on bayberries and poison ivy. Its song, a soft lisping warbling, is easily overlooked in the spring babel of bird song. The spruce-fir regions of the western mountains are occupied by the very similar Audubon's Warbler *(D. aúduboni)* which has a yellow throat and more white in the wing. Young are brownish above. The call-note is a loud *chuck*. The bird shown is a female Myrtle Warbler. Males have a black face and black chest.

Black-throated Green Warbler

Dendroíca vírens

A common summer bird of pine and spruce country, the only yellow-faced and black-throated warbler in the East, and easy to find because of its slow, wheezy song: *zee-zee-zee, saw-see,* given from high in the trees, as a rule. Its voice is as characteristic of the north country in early summer as the whispering pine needles themselves. It has a western counterpart, the Townsend's Warbler *(D. tównsendi)* whose yellow cheeks highlight a black eye-patch.

Ovenbird

Seiúrus aurocapíllus

Throughout the deciduous forest — and the birch-aspen stands that follow fire in the coniferous forests of Canada — this loud-voiced warbler sings from some low branch in spring: *teacher, teacher, TEACHER, teacher.* It is a ground-walker and a ground-nester. Notice the eye-ring, the greenish back, and the lack of bobbing which helps distinguish it from Waterthrushes, another warbler genus you will learn to know after a while, if you persist.

Yellowthroat

Geóthlypis tríchas

An abundant, very widespread, yellow-fronted and (in the male) black-masked warbler of moist shrubbery and weed patches. Female is difficult to tell — as is true of many warblers — but may usually be known from her association with a particular male. Song is a distinctive, quick *wichity-wichity-wichity,* though it varies somewhat from region to region. Do not confuse its name with Yellow-throated Warbler *(Dendroíca domínica),* a distinct species of southeastern forests.

Yellow-breasted Chat

Ictéria vírens

A fairly common summer bird of dense deciduous tangles. Its incredible vocalizations — whistles, cawings, chuckles, etc. — help locate it, since it sings on the wing, and at night. It is our largest warbler, glowing yellow in the breast, rather large-billed, and with a white eye-ring. Strangely, given its tropical affinities, a few tend to winter much farther north than most warblers, except for the Myrtle Warbler.

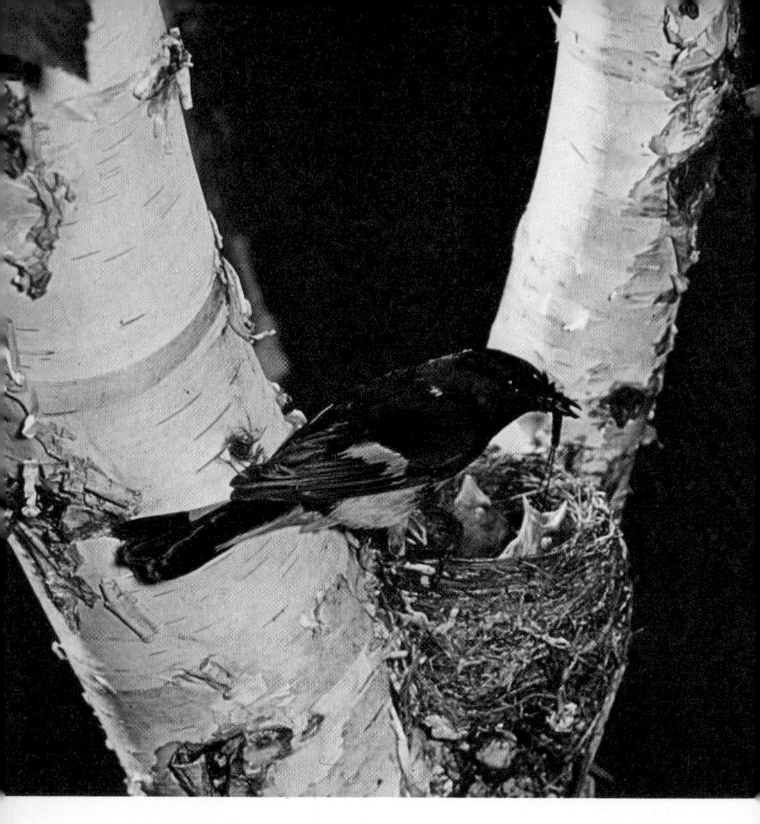

American Redstart

Setóphaga ruticílla

A common, active, startlingly vivid warbler of young deciduous woodland. The males are black above, with bright salmon wing- and tail-patches that are displayed by fanning the tail and spreading the wings. Females are grayish-brown, with yellow rather than salmon patches. One can see, from knowing this bird, why the Latin American name for the whole tribe of warblers is *Mariposa:* they are indeed the butterflies of the bird world.

House Sparrow

Pásser doméstícus

This ragamuffin street bird is often as dingy as the cities it inhabits. It is scrappy, noisy, and equally at home around farms, grain elevators, or palm-lined roads. The black bib sets the gray and brown male apart, but the plain, pale brown female is perhaps best told by her yellowish bill and the pale eye-stripe. Not really a sparrow, nor English as we once called it, it is an African Weaver (a large family of finch-like birds) and is now naturalized around the world.

Bobolink

Dolichónyx oryzívorus

Once very widespread in hayfields, it is now restricted to tall-grass meadows (clover displaces it), but is not uncommon where good habitats occur. "Upside-down" in color pattern — i.e., black below and light above — it has a loud bubbling song and a metallic *chink* note when aloft. Come fall, the males molt to a soft buffy brown plumage, and resemble the females; they are then told from other large sparrows by the pink bill, buffy crown-stripe, and the pointed tail-feathers. In this plumage they are the "rice birds" of the South.

Meadowlark

Sturnélla mágna, S. neglécta

The bright yellow front crossed by a black V, and the white outer tail-feathers quickly identify this quail-sized bird of open fields which often perches on fence posts to sing. It flocks in winter, and flies by alternately flapping and sailing. The Eastern Meadowlark *(S.mágna)* has a slurred *ju-jit-sue* song, while the otherwise very similar Western Meadowlark *(S. neglécta)* has a delightful flute-like whistle, much the best way to tell them apart wherever their ranges overlap. Although these two can be separated by details of marking, song is the safer criterion. The Western Meadowlark is shown at right.

Yellow-headed Blackbird

Xanthocéphalus xanthocéphalus

Few birds glow like the big gold-and-black males of this species, a locally common bird in the cattail and tule marshes of the West. Colonies create a noisy, raucous, squealing clatter. The brown females — especially when they flock with other blackbird species after the nesting season — are easily missed; but although they lack the white wing-patches of the male, they have a clean white and yellow bib, unlike any other blackbird, and this will assure identification.

Red-winged Blackbird

Agelaíus phoeníceus

An abundant, medium-tailed blackbird which nests colonially in cattail marshes or scattered in tall-grass pastures, and often congregates in huge flocks during fall migration and winter. The red-shouldered males are unmistakable. Females and young resemble big, streaky sparrows but have more pointed bills. The male's *cong-ko-ree* call is one of the early signs of spring; and males usually arrive on nesting grounds two weeks before the females.

Common Grackle

Quíscalus quíscula

The common, long-tailed blackbird with a pale eye. In spring, especially, it folds its tail into a trough or boat shape; don't confuse it with the larger Boat-tailed Grackle *(Cássidix mexicánus)* of the southeastern coast. Males are iridescent bronze or purplish; females are somewhat smaller, duller. They nest in colonies in pine or spruce near farms, suburbs, etc. Song is a noisy, squeaky clatter. They flock with Starlings and Redwings in migration and in winter. The smaller Brewer's Blackbird *(Eúphagus cyanocéphalus)* of the West also has a yellow eye but is medium-tailed.

Brown-headed Cowbird

Molóthrus áter

Once a follower of bison herds, and thus called Buffalo Bird, this bird is now common in farmlands everywhere, flocking and often mixing with other blackbirds in winter. It is smaller than the familiar Redwing, and more graceful awing. Females are a uniform mouse-gray (young are buff-throated and have faint breast-streaks). This is the only wholly parasitic North American bird, laying a speckled egg in the nests of smaller birds — vireos, warblers, and sparrows. The song is a wiry, "rusty hinge" whistle.

Baltimore Oriole

Icterus gálbula

Orioles are blackbird relatives but have an even more pointed bill. One of our most colorful summer birds, the Baltimore's clear, fluted whistling, so much a part of spring in the East, seems to be saying emphatically, *Edith, Edith, look here.* The male is the only black-headed orange oriole in the U.S. (others are yellow or chestnut). Females and young are less distinctive, more difficult to distinguish from one another, especially in the Southwest where several other species occur.

Bullock's Oriole

Icterus búllockii

This bird is to the West what the Baltimore Oriole is to the East. Males are black-crowned and black-bibbed rather than black-headed (thus orange-cheeked with a black eye-line), and the wing has a large white patch rather than a simple white wing-bar. All female orioles are for the experts who have mastered many comparative details, and even the most expert will let many pass without committing themselves — which is good advice to beginners.

Western Tanager

Piránga ludoviciána

Tanagers are tree-top dwellers, as colorful but more sluggish than orioles, and with a distinctive, rather "swollen," pale-colored bill that sets them apart from both orioles and grosbeaks. The bill is thus their generic badge. The red head, yellow body, and white wing-bars of the male Western Tanager make it unmistakable. Female and young are yellowish-green birds identifiable by their white wing-bars, pale bill, and black tail. Song is Robin-like, but burry and slower.

Scarlet Tanager

Piránga olivácea

This most colorful bird of the deciduous forest (male unmistakable) is seldom seen unless sought out because it normally stays high in the leafy forest canopy. The slurred, Robin-like song and the metallic two-note call, *chip-chur,* will help locate it in spring and summer. Female and young are yellow-green, with plain blackish wings. Males in molt are a startling, mottled red, green, and black. The all-red Summer Tanager (*P. rúbra)* is a bird of southern woodlands.

Cardinal

Richmondéna cardinális

The only crested red bird, with thick, conical, red bill and black chin-patch. Females and young are reddish-brown (the young with darker bill), but still crested and distinctive. Cardinals (unlike tanagers) are ground-feeders on insects and seeds. They prefer woods borders and hedgerows, so have actually increased in suburban America. The ringing, whistled song is repetitious but never tiresome. In the extreme Southwest there is a gray-backed cardinal with a yellow bill, the Pyrrhuloxia *(P. sinuáta)*.

Rose-breasted Grosbeak

Pheúcticus ludoviciánus

A fairly common but much overlooked species of rich deciduous woodland, suburbs, etc., especially near streams; the unmistakable male is best located by the fast, soft, extended Robin-like song. It shows pink wing-linings in flight. The females are big, streaky, large-billed finches that show yellow wing-linings. The call note is a sharp, distinctive *peek,* a good clue to the presence of these birds once learned.

Evening Grosbeak

Hesperiphóna vespertína

A chunky, golden-hued northern bird whose massive, pale-colored bill gives a bite that bird-banders know only too well. It has large white patches on its black wings, and a short, notched, black tail. A bird of the northern and subalpine spruce regions, it flocks southward when its food supplies are deficient, and then devours sunflower seed at winter feeding stations. Females are grayish, have less white in the wing. The song is like the House Sparrow's chirp, but louder.

Black-headed Grosbeak

Pheúcticus melanocéphalus

The West's counterpart of the Rose-breasted Grosbeak, it is orange-bodied, black-headed, and with the same thick bill and conspicuous wing-bars. Both sexes show bright yellow wing-linings. The song and call notes are much like the Rose-breasted Grosbeak's; indeed the birds are so closely related that they sometimes interbreed where their ranges overlap. The name is of course from the French for large-billed, *grosbec*. A few young birds (in female plumage) are wind-drifted to the East Coast during autumn migration.

Purple Finch

Carpódacus purpúreus

A common bird of open, northern mixed woodlands, and a widespread visitor to feeding stations in winter. Slightly larger than the familiar House Sparrow, the male is raspberry-red all over except for the white belly and brown wings and tail. Notice the well-notched tail and the distinctive *tic* flight note. Females are stout, streaky, sparrow-like finches, but have thicker bills, a white eye-line, and a notched tail (see, also, House Finch). The song of this finch is a rollicking warble, heard at its best in spring mating season.

House Finch

Carpódacus mexicánus

An abundant westerner now naturalized from southern New England to eastern Pennsylvania. The male's red coloring is clearer and more restricted than in the Purple Finch, and the tail is less definitely notched. Females are plainer, darker than female Purple Finches, and lack the latter's white eye-line. The warbling song is somewhat less rich than that of the Purple Finch, and interspersed with occasional grating notes. Except for its attendance at winter bird feeders on the populous East Coast, this bird would be considered too difficult for inclusion in this primer.

American Goldfinch

Spínus trístis

Our small "wild canary" (a term often misapplied to the Yellow Warbler), golden yellow, with black cap, wings (barred), and tail (notched). A late nester in weedy, shrubby fields, it is fond of dandelion and sunflower seed; has a characteristic roller-coaster flight, and calls *per-chic-oree* on the wing. Males are greenish in winter, like females and young, but retain white wing-bars. Small winter flocks roam the countryside, often visit feeding stations. Several other goldfinches occur in the Southwest.

Rufous-sided Towhee

Pípilo erythrophthálmus

A colorful, noisy bird of brush and woods borders. It scratches actively in leafy ground cover, and the white spots at the corners of its longish rounded black tail are conspicuous identifying marks when it departs. Females have the same plumage pattern with reddish sides, but are brown where the male is black. Western birds have white spots on the back. The song is a variable *drink-your-tea,* the last note a dry trill. The call is a slurred *chewink.*

Lark Sparrow

Chondéstes grámmacus

The numerous small sparrows are challenging to identify. Separate them on sight into streaky-breasted or clear-breasted groups. Notice the conical bill, facial markings, wing-bars (if present), length and markings of tail. The Lark Sparrow is a common western field bird, brown, with a distinctive facial pattern and white outer tail-feathers. Females are difficult to distinguish from the Vesper Sparrow *(Pooécetes gramíneus,* which has a white eye-ring) and the female Lark Bunting *(Calamospíza melanócorys),* two other prairie species.

Slate-colored Junco

Júnco hyemális

A plain, slate-colored, white-bellied small bird with pinkish bill and conspicuously white outer tail-feathers. It nests on the ground in northern coniferous forest across the continent; winters over most of the U.S. in small flocks, scratching in brush and wood margins. Immature birds are tinged with brown on the back, have pinkish sides, and may be confused with one or another of the several western species. Song is a slow trill. Of tame disposition, they use a comic little backward hop to clear leaves from a pecking area.

Tree Sparrow

Spizélla arbórea

A subarctic nester that flocks to weedy, brushy U.S. fields in winter. It is a red-capped, gray-brown bird with conspicuous white wing-bars and an equally conspicuous black "stick pin" spot on its gray breast. It is usually seen in flocks and often frequents winter feeding stations, where it may become very tame if approached quietly. At close range, notice the two-toned bill, black above, yellow below. Its pleasant, two-note twitterings become easy to recognize with a little practice.

Chipping Sparrow

Spizélla passerína

This is the small, red-capped lawn sparrow that builds a nest of hair (horse hair or dog hair) in shade trees across the country. Doublecheck the conspicuous black and white lines over the eye and the pale-gray belly for certainty. The song is an equally distinctive, easily recognized, and long-extended series of chips, all on one musical note, like an old sewing machine at work. It seems particularly cheery about sharing its habitats with man, and is well-loved in return.

White-crowned Sparrow (above left)

Zonotríchia leucóphrys

A big handsome gray-headed sparrow with prominent black and white head markings and a pinkish bill. It is a common bird of brushy fields, hedgerows, and even parks and gardens in the West where a resident race occurs. Elsewhere it is an alpine and subarctic nester that migrates to wintering grounds across the Southern U.S., the southeastern coastal plain excepted. This is a more upright bird than the White-throated Sparrow that is better known in the East, and it never occupies the woodlands the latter likes.

White-throated Sparrow

Zonotríchia albicóllis

An abundant winter resident — mostly eastern — in dense thickets within woodlands or woodland borders. It is a much more frequent visitor to winter feeding stations than the White-crown, and perches with a more hunched attitude. Its white throat is clean-cut and distinctive; this and the yellow spot between the bill and the eye set it apart. An excellent singer, its sweet, clear, whistled song, *Old Sam Peabody, Peabody* (or *Sweet Canada, Canada* — since it nests mostly in northern spruce forest) is a favorite north woods voice.

Fox Sparrow

Passerélla ilíaca

This large, bright rusty sparrow is a gaudy version of the Song Sparrow (opposite), though its habits and song are distinctive. The bold rusty streaks of the breast and bright reddish tail and rump, together with the energetic way it kicks up dead leaves — with both feet — make it unmistakable in the East. Western birds are much darker, almost chocolate- or gray-brown, and thus require close scrutiny to avoid confusion with the large northwestern Song Sparrows and dark Hermit Thrushes of the humid Pacific Coast.

Song Sparrow

Melospíza melódia

An abundant, widely-distributed small bird of brushy "neglected" fields and of suburbs that are not too heavily manicured. The prominent breast-streakings run together to form a central spot; the tail is long and brown and is "pumped" up and down as the bird flies off when disturbed. The song starts with three whistled notes, followed by a jumble of trills, *Madge, Madge, Madge, put-on-your-tea-kettle*. Western birds vary much in size and color since they must adapt themselves to such a great diversity of environments.

Index

When picture and text for a bird are on same or facing pages, one index entry is given; when text is on overleaf of picture page(s), two entries are given.

Roland C. Clement, vice president of the National Audubon Society, is also editor of the book *A Gathering of Shore Birds* and a contributor to the Smithsonian Institution's bulletin series, *Life Histories of North American Birds*.